Poets are the bravest

The poems of Wendy Wolff Blumberg

uthentic.

I dedicate this book of poems to The One.

Contents

Foreword

Robert Frost compared writing a great poem to "sitting out in the yard in the evening and having a meteorite fall in one's lap." If that is the case, one would expect Wendy Wolff Blumberg's lap to be overflowing with stars.

I have been collecting the work of my talented friend for many years. Her poems span decades and commemorate a full range of occasions—global and personal, happy and sad. Her words have helped family and friends to celebrate love, beauty and joyous times—a sunset, a picnic at the beach, the birth of a child. She has also given exquisite voice to our grief, after the loss of a dream or the passing of a loved one.

Many times Wendy has slipped me a sheet of paper, saying, in an off-handed way, something like, "This came to me last night. What do you think?" I would read the latest treasure, sometimes laughing, often in tears, invariably deeply moved.

"You have such a gift!" I would tell her. "Your work should be published."

The poet would respond with a modest little shrug. "I just enjoy writing for myself and people I love. That's enough for me."

I would obtain permission to share her latest piece with certain friends and fellow writers—all part of Wendy's steadfast circle of fans—before storing it in a file marked "Wendy's Poems" in bright red ink. Publication, I knew, was only a matter of time. A talent like Blumberg's is simply too dazzling to escape public recognition.

W. Sommerset Maugham was saluting such talent when he said, "The crown of literature is poetry. It is its end and aim. It is the sublimest activity of the human mind. It is the achievement of beauty and delicacy. The writer of prose can only step aside when the poet passes."

Jann Arrington Wolcott
Award-winning Author and Lecturer

Introduction

I wonder what it would feel like today to read the poems I wrote when I was ten and eleven and twelve years old. I began to write poems at summer camp in the Upper Peninsula of Michigan. Every Sunday night we gathered for what was called "Birchbark," where poems and stories or other writings by both campers and counselors were read aloud if they were chosen. I remember the thrill of having one of my poems picked for the readings. The owner of the camp always did this honor. It spurred me on to write more. But these poems were lost in the many moves Mother and I made over the following years. Perhaps the poems never made it home with me from camp. I don't remember.

Unlike wanting to have a poem of mine read at "Birchbark," I have never been interested, or wanted to expend the energy in trying to get the poems published. Whatever time I had to myself, I used for writing them. If I had an experience that moved me in any part of my life, I would try to express my response, my feelings, through writing a poem. Sitting on my bed with a pad of paper and a pen and time alone, feeling the peace of my surroundings, is one of the most contented and joyful times in my life. Even when a poem doesn't work, even when my writing angel can't help me out of a poetic jam, for me this isn't wasted time. It is time I've spent getting to know myself a little better. Failure is as important for me as a poem that has been completed with a fair degree of satisfaction. Actually, there is never complete satisfaction for me. A poem can always be "improved." One just has to stop "tinkering" at some point.

There are people who will always be in my heart, surrounded there with deep and loving gratitude for their support and encouragement for me—and the poems.

The process itself was helped into maturity by poet and actor, Jack Grapes, in his workshops at Beyond Baroque in Venice, California. What a gifted, honest, and gentle teacher he was for me. I am grateful for my time with Jack. How patient he was with me. And in the workshops, I met my friend, Ellen Reich, herself a gifted poet who could send her poems out, and read them aloud at readings with courage and confidence. Ellen encouraged me, and supported me so lovingly and with honesty. I am grateful to her.

There are others in my life who also encouraged me and helped me become more confident that my poems had value. Jann Wolcott, my dear friend, herself an extremely talented writer, always makes me feel I also have talent, even while I still doubt myself. To this day, she harbors a pile of my poems in her files, assuring me she loves having them there. Reva Lear gives me the same encouragement. Lauren Smith, a gifted writer on her own who published two of my poems in her beautiful journal, *Messages of the Heart*, gave me so much in her positive and kind responses to my writing. I am thankful to her. And my daughter, Dina Wolff, who uses her talents for editing and laying out books, created this book, which she insisted was going to be done in spite of my hesitation. How grateful I am for Dina's love and encouragement, her wisdom and expertise in putting this book together. How fortunate I feel.

And then, there is my husband, Stephen. Never complaining when a meal was late or skimpy because I couldn't stop writing. Never too busy to stop what he was doing to listen to a line, a word, a paragraph, and give his input when I'd ask for his opinion. And always honest in his response to a poem. Always loving, even when he might not understand or like a poem. Always encouraging. He even puts "poet" as an occupation on our income tax returns, and any other forms demanding my occupational title. Not homemaker—which I am. But always "Poet." How can I truly express my heart's gratitude to him, except by saying as publicly as this book allows—Thank You.

—July 2001

Children

Letting Go

My children are like migrating birds
One by one they come home
And I hear their laughter
Like unfamiliar birdsong
Clear against the background
Of familiar sounds
My ears open
Recognize   welcome
Listen with pleasure
Until the stillness tells me
They have flown away
Again

-1984

Wendy Wolff Blumberg

Last Child

He says
I'm trying to grow up and be independent
And I don't need you to tell me this
And he takes a knife
That has a blade thick as 22 years
With a thousand words of advice
And a million and more questions
Carved into its handle
Cuts through my umbilical cord
Releases me

-1985

Leaving Home

Andrew puts the book of poetry
I wrote in a workshop
Long ago
Into his duffle bag
It lies down with sweaters
The Way of the Peaceful Warrior
And gloves to keep his hands warm
In the London cold
Andy doesn't say
Look Mother
I'm taking your poetry
Away with me
He doesn't say anything about it
Neither do I
Just thanks inside of myself
That I get to see it there
Before the sides of the bag
Are pulled together
And he zips it closed

-1986

No Beginning . . . No End

When I was a child
I would think about the children
Who would be my children
When I grew up
Who are they
I asked myself
Who will they be someday
And I wondered
Where were they now
They had no names
Owned no gender
But I would feel
Their spirits around me
As my bedroom door
Was closed for the night
And the lights from Chestnut Street
Came through my window
And reached for the covers
Of my bed
When I was a child
I talked with the children
Who would be my children
When I grew up
But no voices interfered
With taxi horns
Or the growls of a Russian Wolfhound
Named Boris

As he prowled the alley below
My window
My bed was a quiet place
Night sheltered it
From the white water flow
Of words
That felt like a thunderous waterfall
Pouring over me each day
Our dialogue was silent
Without rules of time and space
Or the structure years create
Who was the mother
Who were the children
How would I understand
How could I understand
It was a journey of the soul
Through the vastness
Of the mind
Without a beginning
And without end

-1993

Bless My Children

The souls of my beautiful children
Are older
Than the oldest trees
In the Redwood Forest
These souls return again
To earth
And then again
And then again
This time to me
My love for my children
Fills the Universe
Fills it to its farthest
Acre
To the farthest infinity
Then overflows even infinity
Into the soul
Of God

-1993

No Title Needed

My two eldest sons
Cannot get along
They don't speak   don't try to understand
One another
Do not forgive words or actions
That hurt
From years ago
From right now
There is hurt inside me
When one of them
Talks about the other one
I hurt with the knowing
Of how each feels about his brother
Little boys I loved you
Deeply
Grown men   I love you
Deeply
Look inside my heart
You are   each of you
Imprinted onto my soul
I can trace your imprint there
With every pulse beat
As my life's blood
Is pumped through my veins

Wendy Wolff Blumberg

My sons
It feels like a piece of our family
Broke apart
And we
Your sister and brother
Father and mother
Don't know how
To help us mend

-2001

Love Letter
To the Children of the World

Children of the World
You live in my heart
You are in my prayers of love
And peace
Your welfare   your well being
Are in my thoughts constantly
As a stream winds its way down
A mountain
To a river that follows its own path
On a journey that will never
End
For snow comes to the mountain
In winter
And in spring the sun grows warm enough
To melt the snow
Which fills the stream so it can carry
The water down   down
To the river
Which takes this gift of abundance
To every living thing it meets
On its journey to the sea

Wendy Wolff Blumberg

Children of the World
I love you   I bless you
I see you growing up strong
I see you growing up free
I see you filled with feelings
Of love and peace and harmony
Towards everyone and everything everywhere
Which you will use to transform
This world
And Life on earth will be changed
Forever

-2001

Friendship

The Five Minutes at Summer Camp
the Counselors Walked Away

I listen to July
As heat vibrates
In the rhythm of katydids
And I am back at Lake Michigamme
With my childhood friends
Naked as an otter
Cool in the humidity
As we slide off the rocks of Goat Island
Into deep water
Near a boulder padded with moss
Flat as the forest floor
Where my tentmate   Annie
Who cannot swim
Is told to stay
Yet she leans over the edge
Flicking the lake apart
With her fingers
And falls in
Annie's drowning   we yell
Our voices high like the nighthawks
Raucous as the crows
Urgent as loons
When the sun is down
But I am almost five feet tall
And learned the cross chest carry
In a Red Cross life saving class
That ended the week before
So I dive underwater
The way they taught me
Lift Annie's chin above the surface

Wendy Wolff Blumberg

With the palm of my left hand
Hook my right arm around her chest
And pull her to land again
As our counselors come running
They should have remembered
Annie was like the gray squirrels
That breathe only from the earth
And we
Tadpoles halfway to frogs
Agile as minnows
Hiding in algae
Too young to be left
Alone

-1984

Love Letter

Michael   where are you

They found your car
On the edge of a cliff
Above the ocean
Near Daly City
And your brown leather wallet
On the front seat
But no one found you

I think of you often
Even after seven years
You're legally dead now
You know

Once years ago
When we were kids
The sole of your right moccasin
Came loose and flip-flapped
All the way down Michigan Avenue
And the rest of us thought it was funny
To step on it if we could
You in your holey jeans
And plaid wool shirt
And then long after that time
You owned a three-story house in San Francisco
That I cleaned for you when we'd visit
Because you gave up your bed
So Steve and I could sleep together

And I'd hear the foghorn
Blowing from the bay
All night long

Michael
I had a dream about you
Soon after you disappeared
You were young again
You wore a powder blue jacket
With gray flannel pants
Clothes you'd never wear
When you were alive
But I saw your beautiful eyes
And you smiled at me
With nothing to hide
As you sat on the stump of a redwood tree
In the middle of Muir Woods
And there were people around you
I didn't recognize
When I woke up
I was missing you
But understood this was a dream
That connected our two worlds
And you came to tell me
You are alive and well
In yours

-1980

The Subject is Food

My mother and her friend
Talk food
Names of vegetables
I know not
Slip as easily
From their tongues
As raspberry pushups
Slip from mine
They dissect with words
Consistencies of cheeses
Like Mr. Meyer
The science teacher
Dissects frogs
I squeeze my nostrils shut
With my thumb and first finger
Against the smell of either
One

They go on
For hours
I hear their voices
From my room
In the sweat of the
Multiplication tables
How can they
I think
What is interesting
About a recipe for rabbit

Wendy Wolff Blumberg

Stew
Or eggplants from West Halsted Street
In Greektown
Poor souls
They're old
Have nothing to excite them
No other interests in their lives
Except food
Food   food

The other night
Over dinner at a friend's house
I heard about this place
Where they marinate the lamb
At least a week
Or more
Over Souvignon Blanc Chateau
St. Michelle 1979
And chicken cutlet a la Portuguese
And chocolate mousse
We talked food
For hours
It is one of my favorite
Subjects

-1981

My Friend Downstairs

My upside down cat
Lives in the furnace
Steps in and out of ashes
Below chunks of coal
He drinks his milk
From a chipped saucer
And leaves his signature
On my coat
With six brass buttons
Mother paints her disgust
Frames herself in the diningroom
Window
He and I gaze upwards
Studying her
The meaning is clear
Vivid   blunt   terrifying
Like Orazco's revolution
Yet
No war here
He is an upside down cat
And I
Too young to change
Anybody

-1982

Wendy Wolff Blumberg

For Us

When we three turned forty
What a time it was
Around chocolate souffles rising
And red Beaujolais
We threw toasts at one another
Like confetti
Made promises upon promises
Boasts upon boasts
Our switchbacked lives together again
Celebrating forty years
In the same world
Loving like people do
With the crack of wine glasses
Hard against teeth unclenched
To swallow
Allowing our opened throats
Water lily opened   lotus blossom
Opened
For mere hours
To show

In the next room
At eight o'clock sharp
We threw our childhood
Away
Peered into each other's open skulls
Seeing the roads taken
The ones not taken dissolve

Into the champagne
Bubbles rising down through the stems
And out to the dust at our
Feet

For one night
We sang together
Choked our laughter under the lid
Of the watercolor box
Into the tubes of oils
Rolled it under the wheelchair
Below our toes
Shaped its coils into a
Huge olla
Earth toned   sturdy
Deep enough to hold our years

Now
Our thoughts of Michael
Are grains of wheat   bits of corn
We store in the bottom of the olla
As the two of us turn
Fifty

-1983

Wendy Wolff Blumberg

Friends
for Ellen

We sit at a metal table
Astroturf beneath us
Sparrows pick at crumbs from croissants
And sourdough rolls
Other people eat
While we share one hour a week
From our two lives
Over coffee and tea
The sun moves across the patio
Leaves the bouganvilla in shade
We put away our thoughts and ideas
And go our separate ways

-1983

Room 124, Bed B

Bones just bones
So little skin left
To cover his elbows
Shoulders, hips, shins
An eaglet is born
With more down
Than he has skin
His joints sticking out
Like the ribs
Of a broken umbrella

When I rub him with lotion
Left unused by the nurses
On his bedside table
My hands pass over his body
As tho it was a scrap
Of chinese silk
Or the white fluff
Of a dandelion gone to seed
An angel's wing

-1984

Wendy Wolff Blumberg

Jenny

Jenny's pot
Needs a rescue
From the high shelf
On the turquoise bookcase
That hangs over my desk
In the bedroom with the melon painted wall
Of our Santa Fe house
Jenny
A gentle lady from Acoma
Made this pot
Larger than her other pots
But as pots go
Not very big
Jenny called me Darling
And every August
Would sit with her pots
On a side street off the plaza
Being judged not good enough
For a booth inside the boundryline
Of Indian Market
Maybe she didn't care
Her smallest pots sat cradled
In the pockets of an egg carton
Selling for two or three dollars
A pot
I loved Jenny
And would buy her tiny pots

To give friends
At home in California
But then she'd choose
An ornament shaped like an owl
Or a plaque with birds on it
And with both hands
Place it into mine
And say
This one's for you   Darling
Take it
And the price would be the same
As all the little pots
Put together
I'd just bought

One early morning at Indian Market
As the sun climbed over the Sangres
And turned on daylight in the Plaza
Someone came to tell me
Jenny died
Gone in winter from a cancer
That gave her pain
I cried for Jenny
In front of the booths
Facing the Palace of the Governors
Cried in the middle of a crowd of people
Who had never heard her name
Who may have wondered
Over their seven a.m. cup of coffee
"What's eating her"
Afterwards at home near the beach
I went around collecting Jenny's pots
From my friends
Gathered them like the last roses
In October

Wendy Wolff Blumberg

Explained my need
And gave them someone else's little pots
In exchange
No one seemed to mind
Jenny's pots live a quiet life
In California
On the middle shelf
Of an old pine corner cabinet
Nine-hundred miles
From the origin of their clay

Now in Santa Fe
Near the top of the bookcase
Jenny's gift to me
Sits high above my reach
Almost forgotten   unseen
I need to rescue it
Lift it down from there
Bring Jenny back
Into my awareness
Think of her every day
And if I am grown
From that time
What was beautiful
In Jenny
May become beautiful in me

-1987

Sopaipillas and Green Chili Stew

I hear the Guadalupe Church bells
Ringing the sun down
They let go the day
With a hymn of thanksgiving
And then intone the hour
With seven long   slow   clangs
From a clapper on the inside
Of the mother bell
We wait in the parking lot
Of La Tertulia
Lean against the side
Of a red Mustang convertible
And watch people walk through the door
Ready for their sopaipillas
And green chili stew

I think of you
Alone in your one room apartment
In Manhattan Beach California
The quarter moon here is alone
In the southern sky
You sold your rings made of cloisonné
You gave away your leopard pants
And the embroidered vest from India
You've dropped your possessions
Off your back
Like someone running to the edge
Of a lake

With her shoes and shirt and underwear
Scattered up and down the sand hills
Behind her

There are no clouds around the quarter moon
The moon too has nothing
Day is dying quickly
Its end turns the sky golden blue
And the quarter moon rests
In the blue of this golden light
Motionless
A giver of peace

In the parking lot of La Tertulia
Night comes wearing a cobalt cashmere shawl
Your rebozo from Guatemala is made of cotton
The color of winter violets
And a lavender rose
It keeps me warm as we stand and wait
And I am thinking of you
Now another car door slams
Friends are here
A cold wind blows from the mountains
And it is time for sopaipillas
And green chili stew

-1988

Buckle Down To Business

She says
Today is the day
I decided
To start my book
To schedule myself
To discipline myself
So I sat down
And I read *The Times*
All the way
Through

She says
The cancer book
Tells me to talk
To my inner child
So I said to my inner child
What is it you want
And my child answered
Take me to Bullock's
And I said right away
As fast as we can go

-1988

For Jacquelyn

Think back
On a late Midwest fall
The leaves are gone
And the trees have only
Bare branches left
Picture them
As they move in the wind
As they bend
As they reach up
As they lower themselves
To the ground
The truth of trees
Is without leaves

Do not be afraid
Now
To unravel the layers
Of yourself
To use no words
That mislead
To silence
Other voices that cannot sing
The river's resonance
As it carves the canyon walls
As it cuts
Deeper and deeper
Year upon year
To bring its water

To the heart of the earth
And leaves the rocks
Above its bed
Jagged or worn down
And lined like the face of a woman
Who lives a life
And is beautiful

-1991

Wendy Wolff Blumberg

Amiga de mi Corozon

Title inspired by the poem, "Pal of my Heart,"
author unknown, given to me in the late 1970s
by Jacquelyn Fowler

"Oh Wendy
No need for fake flowers
Do hope you haven't searched for them
I want no more
Death does not need things
It stands alone"
              From a letter written by Jackie
              August, 1991

I say to Jackie
Tell me what I should bring you
From Santa Fe
She answers flowers
Those big paper flowers
In purple and turquoise
And the red of my old Mexican serape
So I find paper flowers
In purple and turquoise
And the red of her old Mexican serape
I find them in pink too
And I find them in yellow
Bright as field mustard
Blooming in February
On the hills of San Clemente
And I carry them home
To her
In a brown shopping bag
With Artisanos
Printed in blue on its side

Put on your concha belt
I say to her in my dream
Pull on your suede boots
We'll go to Chichicastenango now
And buy an olla for your flowers
Or we could fly to Peru
And climb the high snow peaks
The ice peaks
Where spaceships land behind midnight
In light from quartz crystals
That reflect a trillion stars
That reflect our years
God will listen to us there

She and I know each other
Across a thousand generations
Of seagulls
Our sons have become men
Our words turn the ocean's breath
Into poems
While a tin angel
Rusting in the night air by her window
Sings a te deum

Amiga de mi corozon
Amiga de mi corozon
I have no more words
I have no song
But here are a few ordinary
Paper flowers
I carried home in a shopping bag
Tell Death to look the other way
Look the other way Death
When I give them
To you

Wendy Wolff Blumberg

Friday After Thanksgiving

She studies the menu intensely
Then orders Welsh rarebit
It arrives as a pool of melted cheese
That covers the oval plate
Strips of crisp bacon
And slices of roasted tomato
Stick up out of the cheese
Like telltale parts of a sunken ship

It is Wednesday
The day before Thanksgiving
In the restaurant of the Little Hotel
On Spaulding Avenue in Beverly Hills
The Geriatric Grill she calls it
And laughs
Every day elderly people come here to eat
With walkers   with canes
Or if they are lucky
With a stronger arm than their own
To lean on

It is men who serve them
Men who have become their friends
Men who came from Mexico
Years ago
And learned English   learned their names
Learned their ways
Who shake their heads

And wink at one another
Over the peculiarities
Over the tastes
Of the old
It is patient judgment
Not without love

She looks up at the waiter
Her plate now resembles a lake
That's been drained
Just residues of yellow sauce
Left clinging to the sides

> Will you be on duty the Saturday
> After Thanksgiving

His smile leaves his face as quickly
As he can pull the blinds shut
Against the sun
When it hurts her eyes
His voice is hushed
As tho they were in a funeral parlor
And he speaks in tones that signal
Respect for the dead

> Oh my dear lady
> We close Friday after Thanksgiving
> We close for good

For her
His words are an avalanche
That will bury the routine
Of her days

Wendy Wolff Blumberg

> For good   you're closing for good
> But what will you do
> Where will you go
> Where will we all go
> Where can I eat my lunch
> Everyday

The waiter shrugs
He holds out his arms
The palms of his hands
Face the square white soundproof
Ceiling tiles

> I don't know   I don't know
> We feel sad
> I feel sad
> Thirteen years I have been here
> Monday new owner say
> Everybody out   everybody out
> We close for good
> Friday after Thanksgiving

It is quiet as a tomb
In the restaurant of the Little Hotel
On Spaulding Avenue in Beverly Hills
She pulls herself up from the table
Offers the waiter her hand
He bows to her
As he takes it in his own
Then she turns away
Walks out the door
Doesn't look back

-1997

Husband

God's Gift

God's gift to me
Those years ago
When we, with summer's sway,
Drew close, was this:
I saw through boyish coverings
The man you would become

And so,
I did not look away

-1966

Wendy Wolff Blumberg

Almost Home

No pilot light
In the eight year-old Lennox
Leaves the house cold
Long before we'd turn the heat down
At bedtime
If you were here to love with me
Now
I'd keep the flannel on
Until we warmed beneath the
Quilts
Slip it off
Over my head
Without shoulders touching air
Warmed skin could touch skin
As it is
Bach's First Harpsichord Concerto
Like the first snowfalls of my children's
Childhood
Settles around me
Above me   upon me
Leaves no part
Uncovered
And keeps me warm
In the dark of the afternoon
At five-fifteen
In late November

-1971

Anniversary Song

Twenty years, love, twenty years
A long way, a long long way.
Fierce loving, love, these twenty years,
A moment from our yesterday.

Twenty years, love, twenty years
Remembered times, beginnings slow.
The binding days we drew together
Twenty years, love, where did they go?

Twenty years, love, twenty years
Reaching towards the dreaming star.
Strength of strength, touch it together,
What I am is what you are.

Twenty years, love, twenty years
The lonely days have since gone by.
The hurting years turned into glory,
No dream lost or let to die.

Twenty years, love, twenty years
A small but precious lot in time.
We've journeyed rather far together,
Ardent with our loving's clime.

Twenty years, love, twenty years
A short way, a short short way.
So look love, to the years yet promised,
Begin again, our wedding day.

-1976

Wendy Wolff Blumberg

Married Life From Hour to Hour

You give me butterflies
Queen Anne's lace and
Wild mustard
The mockingbird sings like a
Thrush
And the sky over the beach
Is blue

There is a stream
A Smokey Mountain brook
To put my feet into
Cold
I can see the stones
On the bottom
Watch the currents
Detour
Around my foot

Once you gave me people
Wonderful   different   forgotten
People
Singing
Where have all the flowers gone
We shall overcome
Along gravel roads
City streets
Country highways

Hand in hand
In parks and temple gyms

Tonight
You bring me
Greasy vegetable chow mein
From
Tai Song's on Sepulveda Boulevard
I can't eat it
I hate
The political campaigns
With your name
Your face
My husband's face
The father of my children's face
My mother's son-in-law's face
Plastered on fences
Stuck on sticks in people's front
Yards
And the reporters from
The Daily Breeze
The Beach Reporter and
The Manhattan Beach News
Are worse
I want to move to Juneau
Away from the the letters-to-the-editors
And my conversations
On your view vs. theirs
As I try to read

Amounts of BHT on labels
At the downtown Safeway

Now
The children have
Graduated
Graduated
Graduated
Graduated

We are
Alone
Alone
Alone
Alone

It will take me an hour
Or so
To remember
The butterflies

-1982

My Husband's Father

We drive from Manhattan Beach to Santa Cruz
Up Highway 101
Just you and me
And it takes us seven-and-a-half hours
To reach Moss Landing
With the old worn out boats
And eucalyptus trees
We pass a graveyard
Somewhere in between
Where tombstones planted on a hill
Like trees in an orchard
Bear nothing but your thoughts
And you speak again of your father's
Death
Which follows you down a road
Of forty years
And I want to tell you
I will listen to you
For a hundred hours
For a million miles
We can even circle
The circumference of the moon
Until you mend

-1982

It's History••••1983

Friends planted a large square garden
In a field below their house
An old adobe off Route 285
That runs from the Taos Highway
To the Gorge of the Rio Grande
Through Ojo Caliente
On the Taos Plains
Rain is on the way here
We can smell it in the clouds
Moving towards us from the Northeast
Feel thunder we cannot hear
In the garden there is sweet corn and zucchini
To be picked quickly now
Before the rain finally comes

This summer in Santa Fe
You cannot walk from La Posada
Down East Palace Avenue to San Francisco Street
And only halfway around the Plaza
We sit down on a wrought iron bench
To watch the tourists   is what we tell each other
Buying pots and heishi
From the Indians under the portal
Of the Palace of the Governors' Museum
Just a year ago
You could have hiked up Canyon Road
Past Old Santa Fe Trail
Climbing through the juniper and piñon

Into the soul of the Sangre de Cristo Mountains
But listen to me
Believe me
When we are in the rented Ford
The mountains are everywhere
And outside the Wheelwright Museum
Standing by the bronze indian chief
Done by Alan Houser
We can feel the mountains breathe
And I am satisfied
I am satisfied

Now in the gray before the rain
You go downhill behind the old adobe
Cross a wooden bridge over the Rio Ojo
To walk through pumpkins and red peppers
Stalks of sweet corn and indian squash
Where the earth is uneven
And the irrigation ditch follows the rows of vegetables
Like a fence that runs along a country road
On the ground you pick up a stick from the cottonwood tree
To use as a staff
And I watch from the porch
As your steps bring you back up the hill again
Before the first drops of rain
Begin to fall

-1983

For Stephen

At the edge of the water
Our feet make patterns in the sand
Yours are block prints
From the looms of Jakarta
Exuberant, bold
And cut deep
With the rhythms
Your leg muscles sing

I want to go back to Meleque
With you
To sit on the beach
Where the children from St. Patricio play
And watch the pelicans dive for fish
While frigate birds float in the air
High above the terns and flying ducks

You walked around the bay
To Barre de Navidad
Alone one January day
Sand crumbling under your feet
At high tide
The lace of fishing nets
Pulled across the beach
And tracks the seagulls made
Washed away
Yet the imprint of your footsteps
Remains deep

And I remember the curve of the shore
The late afternoon sun
On Hotel Tropical
Small and white across Christmas Bay
And I imagine the rhythm of your walking
There
Vibrant, firm
And hear it repeat
In my memory of the wind
As it moved through the palm fronds
In the shade of my jalapa

-1985

Wendy Wolff Blumberg

The Quarrel

She walks out
The front door
Bare feet on cold asphalt
In this November night air
The stars looking brighter
Than other one a.m.s
And no moon
She goes up Blanche Road to Rosecrans
Where the burn-off at Standard Oil
Keeps the neighbors awake
Makes a left turn towards Pancho's
On Highland
Then North all the way to Imperial
Through the tunnel on Sepulveda
Until she reaches Bradley International
At LAX
And a plane to Beijing

She wants to get away from him

Which is impossible
When they're in the same house
The same room
The same bed
For over thirty years
And when the 80 mph artic wind
That can blow inside of her
Dies
She'll want to make love with him
Again

-1988

After the Diagnosis

Do you remember
One warm October Saturday afternoon
In Tijuana
We are visiting our youngest son
His freshman year at San Diego State
When the three of us decide
To drive across the border
Into Mexico
Cars and buses jam the Avenida Revolución there
Trucks squeeze themselves between the buses
And cars
Taxis weave around them all
Like snakes slithering around rocks
Neon lights blink on and off in shop windows
Electric rainbows but no rain
Tourists amble into stores
That sell everything man has ever made on earth
Then amble out again
Restaurants and bars station young feisty boys
On the sidewalk in front of the doorways
To catch pedestrians in their nets
And pull them inside
It is as frantic and whimsical
As Calder's Circus
As Carnival in Rio
As the Macy's Thanksgiving Day Parade
And we three a part of it all

Wendy Wolff Blumberg

Bushwhacking among the leather jackets
Boom boxes and fake Calvins
To hunt for handblown glass goblets
With cobalt blue rims
Thick stemmed and rough pontil markings
On their bottoms
My passion of the year

Oh you are valiant this October afternoon
In crazy Tijuana
You walk when it is hard for you
To walk
When it feels as tho we're enmeshed
In a multitude
Pushing their way out of a bull ring
After the last bull has gone down
But this is your way
You'd walk through a dark woods
A Hansel and Gretel forest
Knowing   believing
The sun is somewhere
Above your head

                    -1989

On a Morning Walk with Stephen

Wind brings Cloud People over the mountains
Who stand like kachinas
Against the blue of the morning sky
They wear kilts and a headdress
Of gray and white feathers
A gift perhaps
From the birds who ferry angels
To other worlds

And they will be motionless
Until the dance begins
Until the beat of drum thunder
Rolls into our minds
Until smells of the high pine forest
Are woven with our breath
Into the rhythm of our heartbeat

Now they move again with the wind
Changing shape as dancers change costumes
And the drumbeaters follow them
Across the sky with their drum thunder
And after the thunder comes the rain

-1991

Truth

This is the truth
You and I are younger than our children
They are strong and understand the world
One by one   if they had to
They could get themselves to Mars
While I
I fight back tears on United's Flight 107
From Orange County to O'Hare
A six day visit to my mother
While you live at home without me

Our bodies are getting older
I say this not because of how we look
I don't care how old we look
But here is a truth
You do care
You wear your new suit
Like a young king wears his ermine robe
On the opening day of Parliament
While I
I wear a denim skirt   a cotton shawl with fringe
From Guatemala
And the two strands of silver beads
I made you buy me
These are all I need
No lusting for Von Furstenburg or Fries
I want to grow into peasanthood
Gracefully

I want our children to say
Those silver beads   that shawl
Mother does wear them well

This   is Truth
You are my love
You are my best friend
Who else would tell me I am beautiful
You are beautiful   You are beautiful
You repeat the words as tho to teach
A child
And I
Being younger than our children
Am gullible
And believe every word I see
In your eyes

-1995
First published in the journal,
Messages from the Heart

Thanksgiving

A lopsided moon rises
Pulls itself up
Into a black rain cloud
Disappears
Leaves behind light
As a token of its presence
Here

You are a husband
I would long for
If you were not already
My husband

What a wonderful world
What a glorious night
This lopsided moon rides the clouds
The air is fresh and cool
Like a clean washcloth
Wet against my face
And there is you
My husband
There is you

-1997

Nature

Wind Poem I

Today I'm afraid of the wind
It pulls at the branches of the eucalyptus
Shakes the tops of the liquid ambers
The mountain ash
Their leaves vibrate like pom-poms
At a football game
I want to stay home in bed

This wind makes a noise like sighs
That never lose breath
I am tense with it
Feel it blow with my nerves
Fill every cell in my body
I want it to stop

Now you've closed the windows
Turned up the volume of the Rams-Bears game
And the jumble of voices I hear from the TV
Comforts me
If I could I would lose this dislike
Of prairie wind
Tell myelf
Prarie wind is just wind
No matter where it
Blows

-1975

Wind Poem II

Today the wind blows
With bursts of unexpected energy
It startles me with its noise
Is there someone behind me
Turn around   look
No one is there
The gusts sound like footsteps
They sound like taffeta
Hoop skirts
Rustling in a waltz
They sound like the rattle of newspapers
Read in bed
Under a dim bedside lamp
Thoughts go back
To times in my life as a child
Alone and scared in dark places
When wind whistled
Through cracks of window frames
A winter howl   a summer sigh
That blew storms into my life
Then blew them away
It is time now
To learn wind music
To dance with both feet
On the ground
Move
Like the branches of a willow
In its rhythm

-1993

Wind Poem III

A chill wind rises from nowhere
And suddenly there is movement
In motionless acacias
Clouds   a quiet ocean
It gives birth to currents of air
Ravens will ride
Finds the open door of my room
Then blows its cold breath over me
Transforming the energies of this hour
As the temperature falls
Changes the mood of my day

It feels like winter is returned
Inside a minute of time
As palm fronds dance on the trees
And white caps race south
Past Carlsbad   past Cardiff-by-the-Sea
I slam the sliding door
Against air that is damp and raw
Air that makes me shiver   makes my body ache
And wonder how the mockingbirds
With such persistant stacatto
Fling their territorial battle songs
Into this wind
That blew in from somewhere
Out of nowhere

-2001

Wendy Wolff Blumberg

Two a.m. on Barranca Road
Santa Fe, New Mexico
August, 1987

A dream
Backs away from my mind
Disappears
Leaves me awake in the night
Like a stone from the ocean floor
Left on land
As the tide rolls out again

While we slept
The full moon moved south
Of the livingroom window
Now
As I stand looking out
I cannot see it
But the garden is almost as bright
As the middle of day
The metal chairs and picnic table
Shine like silver sculpture
And hollyhocks look white
Against the adobe wall

He is asleep
And I am going back to him
And our bed
The world outside this rented house
Belongs to itself
Not me

A moon world
Without breath

Then
Almost to the bedroom door
I stop
A voice I've never heard
But know instinctively
A sound like a warble
Like the treble of a large bird
Comes from the hills
Comes from where there is piñon
And juniper
And low clumps of prickly pear
And I feel the voice floating
Up and up
Into the wake
Of the moon's energy
Until it is gone

This night
Light moves across the garden
To a window
And onto me
I take its gift
Lay it deep
Into my consciousness
And recognize coyote
Singing the moon

-1987

Wendy Wolff Blumberg

Chocolate Moon

Tonight a golden half moon
Hangs upside down
A shape undefined   a broken wedge
Over Dana Point Harbor
It reminds me of when I was a child
And had a chocolate coin wrapped in paper
That I pretended was made of old
Burnished gold
I never understood why
But I broke the coin in two
Gave both halves away
Then tasted chocolate on my tongue
Felt it melt in my mouth
Like a phantom pain
And mourned my loss for days afterwards
Now I watch as the half moon
Sets slowly
Lowers itself down and disappears
Somewhere behind the street lights
On the Point
Somewhere behind the bluffs
Somewhere I cannot follow
As it moves into the water
Moves to another world
But I will bring the light
That old burnished gold paper light
Back to our bed
And cover you with its memory

-1993

So Near   So Far

Four a.m.
Outside the bathroom window
Enough left of the night
To hold Orion in the sky
A personal friend
Introduced to me by my son
When he was nine
For whom I search the night skies
Wherever I am
Lifting my eyes to left   then right
Or straight up above my head
To find it in different places
Different hours
A different season
Now low in the West
Over an unseen ocean
At this time
This four a.m.
From this room
So far from my finite mind
And the window's frame
Oh the wonder of it
The wonder
Orion

-1993

San Clemente Morning

Ravens glide over my head
Wings stretched
Motionless
Call
To the wind
That holds
Carries
Moves them as a cradle rocks
Side to side
Down the hill
Above the rooftops
One with the currents of salt air
That come from the vastness of the sea
Far below

One with me

-1994

Lunar Eclipse

One night
Many years from the birth
Of my soul
I lost the full moon
When its white Christ light
Slowly disappeared
Into the shadow
Of the earth's atmosphere
Leaving only a rim of silver
In the darkened sky

But it returned
That white Christ light
It came back in its own time
As tho a heavy boulder
Was rolled away
From the moon's face
And every leaf of grass
Everything alive in my world
Breathed again

Now I cover my head
With a silk scarf
Close my eyes against its touch
Against the light that moves
In slow procession
Into the dark
And I want to call out

> Mother Father
> Do not leave me
> The moon is gone
> I am alone

-circa 1995

Moon Song

Moon
Come out from behind the clouds
I need your face unveiled
I need the light that pulls
The acacia and myoporum
From the dark
To fall on me
There are pockets of resentment
Closets filled with envy
To clean out
Hidden piles of anger
And disappointment
Negatives of unkind words
Thoughtless acts
To purge
From the pigeonholes
And corners of my mind
I need to clear a path
For Spirit to walk on
Make pure the air I breathe
Cleanse my thoughts
Rearrange my words
Open my eyes to let the sun inside
Of me
Transformation is soul work
Moon
Come from behind the clouds
Unveil your face
We need help
My soul and I

-1995

Sundown

There is a lipstick sky
Above Santa Catalina
The end of this day
There are wild brush strokes of pink coral
Mauve and vermilion
I want to pull closer to me
I want to paint my lips
Smear the colors
Across my mouth
Taste the brilliance
Feel them
On my body
In a dress made of silk
Or crushed velvet
That barely touches the ground
Moves as I walk
Like a slow river in July
And I can see
Scraps of blue tulle
A strand of silver
Through a tear in a stratus cloud
Hanging over the water
Near to a place
The sun
Left this sky
That grows less vivid
Becomes dim
As I write these words
In my notebook

-1996

Wendy Wolff Blumberg

View from a Porch Swing

There is traffic on Bishop's Lodge Road
In Tesuque
Before five this afternoon
Homing trucks and cars
Make noise like running rivers
Swollen with spring thaw
A pregnant horse with the name
Diva
Roams a meadow in front of the porch swing
Where I sit and watch in wonder
As a young dog
With hair the color of adobe mud
Same as Diva
Follows her through the pasture
Stands close while she grazes
Darts away when she lifts her head
Flicks her tail at flies
Unseen from the porch swing
Then comes back
What does he need
This dog who will not leave this horse
Can he sense the coming birth
Want mothering himself
Thunder rumbles somewhere near
The Sangre de Christos
Clouds
Like bed pillows filled with goose down

Move in from the east
From behind the mountains
Dare them
Bring us rain
Bring on the monsoon
Due like the birth
In early July
Over all this
A robin sings its song
Familiar as my own breath
And repeats it again
Again and again

-1998

Wendy Wolff Blumberg

Masquerade

The cat and I
Sit on an old love seat
That is covered with a red Mexican serape
And watch the fog
In late afternoon
Moving across the water
Towards shore
From here on the hill
We look down
On a long low bank of clouds
Different shapes and shades
White and gray
Slowly   relentlessly   stalking   the land
Above the hill
The sky is still blue
The clouds below
A masquerade
Of how the fog will be
When it climbs the hill
Closes in
Our visibility

The cat and I
She with a white fur coat
And black bushy tail
I in less grand attire
Keep watch from the old loveseat

With the Mexican serape
Until the light that made this day
Is gone   swallowed
By the fog
When it swallowed the hill
Now settled for the night
Outside our window
Where no thing moves
Or makes noise
A landscape that is ghostly
Mysterious
From this fog
That masquerades as an early end
To a wintered Monday

-1999

Changes

It is the time of year
Mock orange is in bloom
It is the time of day
The light gives up its final mauve
Pinks and deep coral
As the clouds darken
This is when sweet odors
Of mock orange blossoms
Claim the air
And I am intoxicated
With the smell
They harbor a change
As the season past
Releases to the one beginning
With its gift
That cannot   will not
Last
And every year
Since there is no choice
When it is time
I let go
Let them go

-1999

Parents and Grandparents

Reconciliation

Mother
When he went away and left you
He left me too
And we lived together
You and I
One woman   one child
And I wanted to grow up
To love you both
But you'd come home
From a job that drained you
That made you curl up tight
Inside yourself
I knocked and I know
You tried to let me in
While he went away
And sent letters of love to me
And I cried to live with him
I didn't understand

My best friend told me this
People say your mother
Has a chip on her shoulder
I didn't understand

Believe me Mother
When I tell you
I don't remember
That time in your life

Wendy Wolff Blumberg

When you were ill
When your legs were weak
And you used a cane
When your eyes saw double
And the threat of disease
That would waste you
Hung over us
A girl of fourteen
Awake   awake   whose eyes
Could see   whose brain
Could think
But Mother I don't remember
I just don't remember

Mother
We are healed now
And the years between
Have made us friends
I need you Mother
When you die
No one else can care as much

-1975

Sunset at Long Pond
Legacy

My father's long fingers
Hold the brush again
They move across the canvas
In their own rhythm
Paint the sun coral
As it goes down
Turn it to rust under the water
Against blue of night
Against the blue of Long Pond
Cold, deep
In the light that remains

This belongs to me, I tell him
It belongs to you, he finally agrees

In the studio at Wellfleet
At the edge of the dune
We can smell the ocean
Through the open top of the Dutch door
He steps back from the easel
To study this painting
That has come to me
When he dies

-1979

Fishing

He runs down the sand dune
Slipping sliding down
Flings his fishing line over his head
A school of dolphin near the shore
Dive in and out of the water
I can't believe it
Father wants to catch
One

He runs down the beach
Races with the dolphins
They play with him
Tease him
Never losing pace
His feet
Pound the shoreline
Keeping up
Until
Far down the beach
He loses breath
Falls back
And they swim
Away

-1981

I Dream of Losing Father

I am nine years old
The war has begun and my father
    is drafted
Even if he and Mother are divorced
I get to see him every week
It is very different than when
    we lived together
I suppose I should be used to his
    absence in everyday life
But he is drafted and I am frightened
Imagining that when he goes away
    I will never see him again
Even tho he smiles at me and says
    he is too old to fight

It is the first dark winter of the war
I walk the dog and look up at the sky
Watching for bombs to come tumbling
    down from the clouds
Tho mother says the fighting is far away
Father leaves for the war before dawn
    one winter morning
He leaves from the Seneca Hotel
    with a large group of men
I can see the Seneca Hotel from my bedroom window
The doorman bows as he opens the
    car doors
Father tells me he will wave
    as he marches away and

Wendy Wolff Blumberg

I promise I'll be at my window
    to wave back at him
I fall asleep sometime in the night
When I open my eyes the sun is high
    above the Seneca Hotel
He has marched away in the dawn
    hours ago
I haven't been able to stay awake
    and I haven't been able to wake up
And I feel I have missed my last chance
    of ever seeing him again
Well he didn't die in that war
    but he didn't come back when it was over
He moved two thousand miles away
    and I visit him once every year
At sixteen I wear lipstick
    and he walks right by me in the station

-Published in *South Bay Magazine,*
July 1981

Lost Words

You made me feel at home
In the house where a British soldier
Was hanged from a tree
In 1777
The low ceilings and wood floors
You were always having to repair
And the white walls with the paintings
Mostly done by you
Gave me the illusion that I knew you well
And you knew me
That we loved each other
Is certain
But we lived in different areas
Of our minds
Your words
Flew far over mine
And were lost
Now I am the age
You were then
And although it is too late
To find them
I listen to you
Still

-1982

Wendy Wolff Blumberg

With Nana

In a memory of childhood
She leans over my bed
She lifts the blanket cover
And puts her hand between the sheets
Then
Flutters her fingers in the darkness
Where I sleep at the bottom

It is Wednesday
The nurse has half-day out
Nana comes to wake me from
My nap
Pulls up the window shades
Sees the place near my pillow
Where I tear the wallpaper
Off the wall
Says nothing

The peacocks
At the Lincoln Park Zoo
Wail
I cover my ears with my hands
To muffle the noise
As she takes peanuts from a paper bag
Holds one in her fingers
Between the iron bars
And waits
The ducks come to snap the peanut

From her fingers
Like the cook jabs potatoes
With a fork for baking

She says I may have a peanut
To feed the ducks
Holds the paper bag open for me
But I am afraid to put my fingers through
The iron rails of the fence
She laughs
Says
Don't be a goosie
They won't bite

It is Wednesday afternoon
At the Lincoln Park Zoo
She wears a woolen suit
And ruffled blouse
Her gray hair under a feathered hat
I remember the feel of her cotton glove
In my hand
And the sound of her shoes
On the pavement

-1982

Wendy Wolff Blumberg

Hands

Grandmother is old, she is frail
I am one-hundred years
She says, though only ninety-seven
Her fingers trace patterns on the lap robe
And she watches as they move
To the right, to the left
I am nervous, she says
I am nervous
Then her hands lie open
On her thighs
Palms touching the blue wool
She lifts them up, then down
Slowly, again and again
I sit in a chair
Close to the one that enfolds her
Cover her hands with mine
And feel the flutter of her nerves
Like a thousand butterflies
That struggle for release
From their cocoons

-1982

In the Eye of the Red Wind

Grandfather lies dying in his hospital bed
While Grandmother reads aloud to him
The 23rd Psalm   over and over
I don't know what to do with the corridor
Where I stand outside his room
The tile floor makes a hollow echo
Under my penny loafers

It's as though Grandfather's bed is at the end
Of a long tunnel
A patch of white
Far from the walls I can touch
On either side of me
And I hear Grandmother's voice
As she leads him to still waters
And feel the breath of a blue wind
Blowing

His is the first time I look at the colors
Of death
His white face   white hair
A white sheet covering his thin body
And then the grays
In his room where Grandmother sits beside him
A gray sweater over her shoulders
The gray light that leaks from behind
Closed venetian blinds
And the dark dark gray of the hall
Where I wait outside his door
Afterwards   white again

Wendy Wolff Blumberg

Snow on the cemetary ground
And black
Black clothing   black bark of bushes
Dormant in November
The gray-black clouds of an approaching storm

This grandfather   my grandfather
Would not like this white   these grays
The black
His colors were vibrant
Twinkling blue eyes   the yellow of jaunty steps
It was he   afterall   in the morning of childhood
Who taught me laughter
In the eye of the Red Wind

                        -1982

Salt Air

The ocean moves past me
On the Hermosa pier
Slaps the concrete pilings
On its way into shore
And pulls me backwards
Into a Pennsylvania summer
Where on an afternoon
Damp and heavy as a cow's tongue
I sit in the middle of a brook
Cool beneath a parasol of willows
That hang motionless
Over the banks

Father doesn't know I am here
With the Guernseys
Listening to the water
Lap against their sides
Listening to the meadowlarks
The katydids
And the mouths chewing their cuds
Until the sun goes down behind the elms
That line the rise above the farmhouse
And I hear my father's voice
Calling to me
Woofie   come   Woofie where are you

Now there is vermilion
Where the sun finishes this day
As I walk back across the sand

Wendy Wolff Blumberg

It reflects in a thousand windows
That face the sea
My father's voice is quiet again
And in his silence
The gulls throw their cries
Into the wind

-1986

Journey

Mother
I have traveled a long long way
From you
Would you know me?
It is true
You charted the country
That was my childhood
Made maps leading me
To roads I had to find
Detours to bypass
Dangers to avoid
You drew heavy doubled lines
In red ink
Which curved   switchbacked
And swiggled like snakes
To mark places where honesty
Good manners
And the ability to obey
Could take me
You were a good mapper
But I went underground
Then flew to the moon
And around the constellations
Climbed mountains
Swam oceans   rivers   the seas
Got lost   got lost
Searched for other roadmaps

Wendy Wolff Blumberg

In my mind
Studied the web of feelings
In my soul
To untangle and rewind
Rewind and rewind
In sunset colored yarns
Of scarlet   mauve   purple
And deep gold
It can never finish

Mother   Mother
I will come back
To where you are
But how will you know me?
Will you know me?

Dedicated with love
to my daughter, Dina Wolff
-1991

To Alice
(Mother's Day, 1991)

My mother's years
Fall around her like a velvet cloak
Cover her with folds of silken thread
Of gold, deep blue, of burgundy
Like the colors of cloth in a painting
By Rubens or Rembrandt
But it has a lining of woven straw
This cloak of velvet
That can scratch and tear the skin
Straw on one side, velvet the other
The fabric of a life
The way it is, my mother says

And she gave me straight hair
And thin ankles
And she gave me love
She gave me the markets of Guadalajara
And Oaxaca
And she gave me the truth
Of her own self

One July we are very young
We eat lobster bisque together
And watch the seagulls live their lives
On the pier in Monterey
As the sun is going down
Back at the restaurant in the Monterey Hotel

Wendy Wolff Blumberg

The waiters are on strike
All the others from the tour bus
Cross the picket line
But, my mother says, not us

Now hawks glide in the wind
Over the roof of my house
This house where my mother has never been
And I tell her how they rise up
And soar
How they dip with their wings outstretched
And sway into the currents of air
And I tell her that her years
Fall around her like a velvet cloak
And she is beautiful

-1991

When Mother Died

You who were with me
In this life
You whose days and nights
Were woven into mine
The shuttle of hours moving through
The minutia
And the large events
That could bring pleasure
Or confusion
Or move us to a place
Of tears
You who have gone to a different plane now
Another realm
Are remembered

When mother died
I felt an intense brightness
All around me
She and I lived inside this light
For three days and three nights
Before she left
All the baggage she'd carried
Dropped away
Only her essence remained
It was as though the other side of life
Lifted its veil long enough
For my spirit and her spirit
To say goodbye   for now

Wendy Wolff Blumberg

There is an invisible kingdom
Unseen   unheard   but known
In the heart and through the mind
When Mother died
The kingdom's gates opened for her
And I felt the incredible
Joy

-1999

Grandfather Aaron

My father's father
Dies before I am born
Collapses at the dog races
And it is told to me
By Cousin Peter
That before he goes his way
He says to his friend
Who is bending over him
      Boy—I sure went to the dogs
      Tonight

It is the first time
I ever hear of this
For most of my life
He is only a name
Grandfather Aaron
For most of my life
He is just a photograph
A man at ease on a horse
Face turned to the camera
At peace   serene
Riding with no awareness from me
Down the years of my life

Today
I am older than Grandfather Aaron
Who dies at sixty
Today
He is a man whose existence

Wendy Wolff Blumberg

Is like a book collecting lint
On a top shelf
Unopened   unread

When I am a little girl
My father tells me this
        Your Grandfather Aaron
        Would have loved you
        He would have played with you
        Given you horsy-back rides
        You'd have been his delight
But Grandfather Aaron isn't here
And Father's words mean nothing to me
Grandfather Aaron rides on
Unnoticed through the years of my life
Until now
When it is too late to ask
When no one is left
Who knew him
Or would talk with me
About him
Tell me stories of this man
Who could say
As he lay dying
        Boy—I sure went to the dogs
        Tonight

                        -1999

Potpourri

Brothers-in-law

My two uncles
Mother's brother
Her sister's husband
Call each other son
I can hear them saying
How's the property at State and 69th, son
Doing better, son
How'd the golf go, son
Fine, son, just fine
Even Father
While married to my mother
Is son
A most unson like man
But in the days before the war
When Grandfather walks briskly
Swings his cane
Tips his bowler hat
Buys me balloons
Every Sunday
From a man we call
Balloon Man
In the days I go to sleep at night
With both a mother and a father
In the house
In these days
My uncles and my father
Call each other
Son
I think it is the name they use for
Brother

-1971

Wendy Wolff Blumberg

The Mobile

C
a
l
d
e
r

And the perfection
                of
                    balanced shapes
                                taught me
                    with ever
changing form
            that
                empty air
                    is
                empty only
                        to the unknowing
                                eye.

Calder,
And the movement of things
Stirred into constant motion,
Remind me that I understand
What I don't understand.

Calder,
Will the fulfillment of space
And the vibrant movement of ideas,
Ever reach the stagnation of humanity
And set it in motion

                ?

                    -1973

The Party

His toes on the piano keys
Play sharps and flats
Bass chords past middle C
To the treble clef

The roller spins laughter
Pushes keys up and down
In rhythm with the toes

Santa Claus dances in a red shirt
White Huck Finn hair uncombed
Round stomach like Baba Au Rhum
On the table with roast turkey
And ham

His mobile turns in drafts
From dancers and songs
Red   Blue   Yellow
Move round and round

Feet stomp on the oak floor
Unpolished   uneven   old
My father's paintings move on their nails
And the walls slant downward
To the road

-1974

Wendy Wolff Blumberg

Walking Straight Into It

In dreams I still see firefighters
Combing the sides of Braintree Mountain
Balls of lantern light appear and disappear
Through the pine trees, through oak and birch
The low fern
No outline of Braintree Mountain
Leans against the night sky
And I see nothing but lights
Moving, always moving

Braintree Mountain
A thousand miles from the polio virus
Mother, my own bed
Across the meadow of rock and low grasses
Above White River
And the wasp nests of summer camp
From cabins on the lips of the meadow
We watch cycles of the mountain's life
And the path of Orion and the Dippers
As they move overhead

Old Elijah Sims brings maple syrup
For our breakfast
Tells us stories of the Green Mountain Boys
And fires he fought on Braintree
Long before we are born
I imagine flames larger than the Merchandise Mart
Tall as the Palmolive Building

And high as the Lindbergh Beacon
Burning the trees and grasses
The honeysuckle vine
Leaving nothing but charcoal, nothing but ashes
Everywhere

Sometimes
Not certain, but afraid
We see wisps of smoke above the pines
Or rising over timberline on the western flank
If it's false alarms they come anyway
Invisible by day, lantern eyes at night
And I love these unknown men who prowl the mountain
Just over the river from my flannel sheets
And bottom bunk bed

Blind Molly with me on her back
Won't hurry
Steps slowly through laurel and red clover
I look up at gray clouds that mask the dry woods
Where lightning strikes on Braintree Mountain
Shake the reins and cry, Run Blind Molly
But the rain can't wait
It falls from the mist down the mountain's side
Crosses White River, reaches the meadow
And with the wet earth smells coming to meet us
I let the steady rhythm of her hooves
Carry us straight into it

-1975

Night For Day

This child of night
Cradles the evening star in her mind
And carries it across the day
Not in darkness as it could imply
But as crystal, as a brightness
Culled from prisms
Then she reaches past the sun
And pulls the Infinite closer

I want to mold the mauve of dusk
Into midnight
And weave the coral of daybreak
Into the deep parts of myself
The moon sets before the first dove calls
And the rhythm of my breath
Sings with the tides

-1976

Invitation

It is I
Who invited the cowbird
Here
To build her nest
Under a tarpaulin
Beneath the oleander
You blame me
For inviting her in
You
Who can see dust
On a crystal prism
Rubbed with chamois
Since 1962

I watch the cowbird
Lift the lace of my antimacassar
From the wing chair
Trail it through the hallway
To the tarpaulin
Beneath the oleander
She pushes the antimacassar
Under the tarpaulin
Pokes it out of sight
With her beak
Lies down with her eyes closed
Sleeps for eleven days
And twenty hours

Wendy Wolff Blumberg

I know now
Your are right
There is nothing anyone
Can do about
Cowbirds

I should have listened to her sing
First

-1982

Mourning Lucky and Poochie

Here is the backyard
I keep the kitchen door
Locked
Pretend
There's a time of day
Dogs walk
Run seagulls
Off the shore
Crawl under evergreens
Or camellias in bloom
Invisible

The spigot drips into the
Dish
Is empty
Dustballs
Like tumbleweed
Catch the fence
Roll away
I listen for sounds
Backlash from five o'clock
In the afternoon
Growls
Indignant
Disgusted
Have gone away
Motorcycles   copcars   Volkswagons
Metermen   noisy children   paperboys

Unknown animals
Unknown humans
Unknown footsteps
All pass by
Without notice
Without comment
Without sound

They lived the corners of
My life
For me
Without them
I am only a
Circle

-1982

A Paris Play

Now
I'm going to tell you the story
Of my coming home to Paris
Where I've never been before
In this life

This I remember
It begins with rain
We dance with it over Le Pont St. Michael
Gray clouds hide me from Le Louvre

The truth is certain places nudge my soul
I grab at them too lightly to hold on
This one slides down my gullet before I can hold it back
I feel the passion of recognition explode

Dina is with me in this play
She leads me down an alley in the Latin Quarter
We are on the left bank of the fourteenth century
A white dog scratches at the door
Of our hotel

On the way, I gather faces from the lights of shops
From chairs in cafés, from flower stalls
Arranged on lips of narrow streets
I gather voices, the sound of words, language
Feet on cobblestones, the late afternoon air
On my cheeks
Pull them into my mind as fishermen
Haul nets full of fish onto sand

It is the first hour I am here
A man runs to a gendarme on the corner
Waves his arms, points his finger
Disappears with the gendarme down our alley
We are on the left bank in the fourteenth century
A white dog is scratching at the door
Of our hotel

Daughter, let the bathwater run
She is not a child to be bathed by her mother
Her childhood recedes again
She is a woman like myself
It is she who has brought me to this city

A blue slate roof lies across from our beds
Stone walls below it so close
We could brush them with a long handled broom
We are taking off our clothes
The bathwater runs
It is time to draw the blue flowered curtains
I go to the window and look down

Center stage directly below
An archway leads into the old apartment house
Under the blue slate roof across from our beds
The gendarme is there
Then four, ten, twelve gendarmes
Dark uniforms, box caps, visors hiding eyes
They talk in twos
Split, regroup, talk in threes
Gallop, canter, ride on bicycles

Into our alley, up to the archway
Twenty, thirty, forty gendarmes

Now comes their leader
He wears a black suit
Orders gendarmes through the archway
Orders them around on the street
Orders a passage cleared
An ambulance creeps into the alley
Comes to a stop
A stretcher rolls through the archway
I am stuck to the window
A magnet against a brass pot
Can't move
Dina's bathwater laps around her body
I hear it behind me
A man in a loose, white jacket
Parks his bicycle behind the ambulance
Walks slowly through the arch
I slam the blue flowered curtains shut
She is too young to witness this death

On my knees under the window dipping into my suitcase
It is my turn for a bath
She runs the water for me. It rushes
Into the tub. I won't look at the ground
I promise myself I won't look
We talk about summer in Aix-en-Provence
The lake at Annecy, spring wine
But it is too late for me, I can't help myself
I look out again, I look down
I look right into his face Jesus Christ God Almighty
I look at him

Wendy Wolff Blumberg

He is the color of dust
He is wrapped in orange plastic
He wears a red stripe under his chin
He is put into the ambulance
He is taken away
He is very young and my love for him
Finds its place in my soul
Dina comes out of the bathroom
Hot water is ready for me
In our hotel room
Life goes on

Awake in the middle of night
Empty streets, quiet after a storm
This is Paris, entangled in my guts
Beloved as a child at my breast
Music that weeps deep inside of me
Touches my heart, lightly, lightly
This is the story of coming home
To a place I've never been before
Dina is with me
Once again

-1986

At the Safeway

She must be lonely

She pushes her grocery cart
Between the aisles
At the Safeway
Slowly
Looking for a familiar face
As she reaches for fresh brussel sprouts
Or a bottle of Pine Sol
So she can talk

She says
My daughter gave a party
And two-hundred people showed
It was for that assembly man
You know
I forget his name
He's running for the senate now
The one in Washington, D.C.

Polite smiles answer her
Heads nod good-byes
From the frozen foods
I hear her voice all the way
To the laundry detergents
And kitchen cleansers
She says
You should have been there
Two-hundred people showed

Wendy Wolff Blumberg

He's a nice man
But I forget his name

I plunk the rainbow sherbet
Into my cart
And hurry away
Am ashamed of myself
But not that lonely
Yet

-1987

Dark O My Moon

My father's son
Lives on the dark side
Of my life
No whole or half
Or quartered pieces
Of a day
A month   a year
Bring him to my table
Leave his woolen sweater
The one he brought
From Ireland
Hanging in my closet
As he plays his banjo
By the fire
Or gives me words to dig
Into his memory
Of our father
But on a night
When the moon is full
And the sky clear
Its light is everywhere
Even under rocks
Even behind stone walls
Even across the years

-1988

Wendy Wolff Blumberg

Priority

An article in the metro section
Of the *L.A. Times*
Describes a building
One story   downtown   rundown
Fenced-in   city owned
Empty
For around $300,000 dollars
Which nobody seems to have
It could be a shelter for the homeless
Who climb the fence to sleep there
Anyway

On the same page
An ad from Bullock's Wilshire
Describes a necklace
Of eighteen caret white gold
With brilliant pear-shaped diamonds
And what looks like
One very large emerald
The asking price is
$300,000

-1989

Blue

At ten o'clock this morning
A sky   blue and uncluttered
Brings other blues
In other times of my life
To the surface of my mind
This sky is like a lake
Known to me
From childhood
Especially so at sunrise
When the air was still
When no leaf or blade of dune grass
Moved
Before bird or insect born to daylight
Was awake
And the blue water seemed to sleep

My grandfather's eyes
Were the blue of this sky
He was not a tall man
He wore spats and a bowler hat
Swung his cane
As he strolled down Michigan Avenue
Every Sunday
When bronchitis put me to bed
He'd bring a single red rose
Smile
Whenever he looked at me
And I remember him
Remember his blue eyes
Alive again
In the eyes of Jay

Wendy Wolff Blumberg

The eldest son
Of my eldest son

And there was the blue of a wool dress
Grandmother wore
Its left side scorched
By a burner on a gas stove
As she warmed a can
Of Campbell's Split Pea Soup
When she was ninety-three
Her children saw that blue wool dress
Told one another
Mother almost set herself on fire
Never allowed her to live alone
After that

In my life
There have been blue bells and blue eyes
Blue buttons on blue dresses
Blue ribbons
Blue words made by blue ink
On blue paper
One mountain bluebird
In a piñon pine
On this morning around ten o'clock
A pure blue sky
Deep and unfathomable
By two in the afternoon
A gathering of clouds
A different sky
Different thoughts
Different colors
A different life
A different mystery

-1994

Poets are the bravest

Cocktail Parties

Please
Do not invite her
To cocktail parties
She doesn't know how to make small talk
With strangers
Her mind wanders away
Flits into another room
Flies out a window
Or through the door
Leaves a vacancy
That shows in her eyes
Unfilled by weather reports
Stock market temperature
Theories of political prophecy
She doesn't drink liquid from bottles
Sitting side by side
On top of white clothed tables
Doesn't eat canapés made of cream cheese
With anchovies on marmalade
And if she meets a familiar face
Voices of other guests
Sound to her
Like a chorus that practices
Different parts of different songs
All at the same time
Drowning out her tries
For intimacy

Wendy Wolff Blumberg

She dislikes standing
With a glass of ginger ale
In the middle of so many people
It makes her think of a herd
Of cattle
Who must wait to be loaded onto
Cattle cars
Crowded together
In a holding yard
Whisking their tails at flies
And she wonders about them
Worries
If they have a thimble full
Of knowing
Where they will go
And why
So please
Do not invite her
To your cocktail parties
She doesn't like crowds
Does better in small groups
Is great one on one
Can't change now

-1996

There are Times . . .

Perhaps on an afternoon
As the house is quieted
And my mind turns away
From the loose change of thoughts
Which jangle around the running
Of my life
A door opens to a place
Inside myself
Where the voices of my children
When they were little
Speak to me
And I listen and try
To learn from what they say
Whether or not I led them well
From where they began
To where they are now
Oh   I knew then
I had to harvest these voices
Had to imprint images of their faces
And put to safekeeping the way it felt
To carry them in my arms
It goes so quickly
Grandfather and Grandmother are long dead
Father also gone
Mother is an old old woman
My children are the ages
Of their father and myself

When we were young
Now in the quiet
Of afternoon
I can feel our lives moving swiftly
Like a log raft down a river
Past the high and low markings
Of the tide
And I want to hold them all
Close to me
I want to look into their faces
Hear the timbre of their voices
Feel their skin against my skin
Before the jangle of thoughts
Comes back
Before the door
That opens inside me
Closes again

-1996

Shades of Gray
(A Poem of Gray Adjectives)

Today
Is a gray day
There are gray clouds
There is rain falling
Soundless
The ocean
A sheet of gray glass
No boat could slice its way
Through
While the horizon hides
Behind a curtain of gray fog
And in my imagination
Reaches forever
Catalina is also gone
Perhaps
Never to be seen
From my window
Again
It is a day
Of gray patina
Grays of an old pewter
Jug
Haunting   mysterious
Beautiful

And then
Gray

Wendy Wolff Blumberg

That feels dense   dark
In my mother's anger
In her despair
Mother   mother
I do not choose to follow your path
I do not
But give me your gray
Words
And I will turn them
Into doves
White   like the pearls
My father gave you
While the sun lowers
Through the clouds
Through fog
And sets the gray
On fire

-1997

Hanging On

There are dead people living in my address book
Their telephone numbers and places of residence
Have their own locations behind the alphabetical
Headings
Although for some
There are many lines here and there
Where their names and addresses have been crossed out
And new information concerning their whereabouts
Squeezed in
They mingle without difficulty
With those who are alive and well
And it is almost impossible for me
To consider removing them from this reference library
Of my life
As long as I can see their names
As I find my way through the pages
It feels as if they are still here
Available for conversation   for connection
Of our voices
For a reaffirmation of our love for one another
Even as I understand
This cannot happen anymore
And in truth to myself

Wendy Wolff Blumberg

I know when their names are removed
It will be like a final goodbye from this life
And so   dead people are still living
In my address book
It takes a long time
To let them go

-2001

Spirituality

Totem

The sun is an hour
West of noon
No wind to lift the raven
Yet she comes to me
Over the Sangre de Christos
Glides on a current
Of turquoise air
A whisper perhaps
Left from the night breeze
That dies before morning
In the sand of the arroyos

She weaves wisdom
On a loom
Made of Bosque honeycomb
And tiny clamshells
From the red clay of Abiquiu
And the fabric
Of this day
Is a signpost
To my millennium

Now the sun is down
The Jemez have turned indigo
Crimson clouds are gray again
Smells of piñon and juniper
Of damp earth
Grow stronger

Wendy Wolff Blumberg

When daylight disappears
And the road home
Is short
As it leads me straight
Into my own self

Then the raven
Black as midnight
With no moon
Brushes the dark
With her wings
And is gone

-1990

Totem II

Raven dies on the road
But not alone
Spirit of the wind
Alive in the chamiso
Alive in the juniper
The aspen
Golden clover
Brings rain
To dampen the dust
On the earth
On the red earth
Where he lies

She will bury him
By her medicine wheel
In whorls of cedar smoke
And white cotton
Gray clouds run to Taos
Above her head
Lightning comes
Without thunder
To find deep cobalt blue
In the black of his feathers
And his wings are messengers
Of what she has forgotten

He will go to the pines
He will go to the tall pines
Where air is cold
Sweet   thin
Clear as herkemers
And he will fly there
Again

-1991

Wendy Wolff Blumberg

Sister

Go into the light
Open eyes that no longer
See the sun or recognize
The moon in a familiar world
I have been told
By a feeling inside myself
Not a solid source of knowledge
For some people
But powerful to me
That there are no walls
Of time or space or even of the mind
We will not lose any dear thing
That lives within our memory
Everything that is of love
Goes with you
Everything that is of love
Remains with me
Unencircled   unenclosed   connected
Through all our lives
By a silver cord
That reaches to the Infinite

-1992

Child of Light
To Jeffrey

Child
Heal yourself
Dig a deep trench
Inside of you
To reach your soul
Release its light
Follow the rivers and byways
Of your blood
The roadmap of muscle
And bone
Pull your light up
To the surface of your mind
To your home
Inside the secret rooms
Of your heart
You are a light
Shining in a vast universe
Recognize the power of your
Being
Child
Heal yourself
Now

-1996

Wendy Wolff Blumberg

Meditation

The wind's breath
My breath
In rhythm one with one
Roll the ocean past Catalina
Blow blue green water
East of Avalon
And row after row of waves
South toward Encinitas and Del Mar
Clouds like cottonweed
Coral-hued
Low as ravens fly
And under a canopy of cirrus
Dark as old pewter
Rubbed with shammy
Follow
I sit on an oak bench
In movement   a fugue
With sea   cloud   sky
Breathing in   breathing out
Breathing in   breathing out
Breathing the sun down
Breath by breath
Into fog
Shaped like a distant mountain range
A mirage of the Himalayas
With a thin gold cord
Rising behind the fog

To lie along the rim
Of its jagged peaks
A dream of high snow fields
On Annapurna
Where the flash of a snow leopard
Is caught in the blink of an eye
And am one with The One
In the sun's last breath
As the gold and the coral
Without light to sustain them
Change again to gray

Breathe the day out
Breathe the night in

Breathe in   breathe out
Breathe in   breathe out

Breathe

-1997

Wendy Wolff Blumberg

Liken unto God

Rocks talk to me   wherever we meet
In a variety of gardens
On a beach
Walking down the road into town
They speak to me
I feel their voices
Hear them with my heart

Boulders call from hillsides
From sculpture gardens carved by glaciers
All colors   all sizes
Shaped by moving ice
Millenniums ago

Stones soothe me   pebbles please
Large and small they reflect cloud shadow
And sunlight
Transform themselves under the moon
Whisper their ancient births
Give secrets to those who know
How to listen
How to look   really look
And they comfort me   they comfort me
I can rub my hands over a smooth back
Trace a jagged edge
With my finger
Touch their wisdom   trust their age
And know

All history   every history
Because everyone   everything on earth
Creates a history
Matters not to them
Like God
They live in unconditional acceptance
That what is
Is

-1998

Wendy Wolff Blumberg

Ketchikan

I remember the mist
In Ketchikan
Like a curtain around me
Soft as old lace
Diaphanous
Mist that is rain
Rain that is mist
Moving as I move
From the shore
To the heart of town
Where native children
Dance
I remember the smell
Of wet earth
The smell of yellow
And red cedar
The pines
A sound like whispers
As drops of rain
Fall through their branches

I remember the totems
In Ketchikan
Regal   old
A hundred or more years
Old
Their paint faded
Weathered to gray

Standing where they are raised up
As generations
And the seasons pass
Until they fall
Clan emblems of the Raven
Of Eagle
The Whale and Bear
Carved out of the trunks
Of red cedar
From visions
And the magic of myth
Mysterious   mystical
Too powerful for who
I am
And from where
I have come

      Let me in
      Let me know you

      Not this life

They answer
From the mist
From the rain
In Ketchikan

-1998

Wendy Wolff Blumberg

Transcendence

They dance the harvest
Under the sun
Dance thanksgiving
Under clear acrylic blue
Like a mural of unmarred sky
No brushstrokes showing
In the shade of an old cottonwood
An infant wind cools my face
A sound of pueblo drums
Elders chanting sacred words of prayer
And the sudden howl from a koshare
Fill the world around me
Even to where my heart
Beats its own
Rhythm
As the dancer's slow steps
Their eyes to the ground
Create
Circle upon circle
On the red dust
Of the plaza floor

This is the time of year
The aspens and chamiso
Turn to gold
Wild asters bloom along roads
To San Juan Pueblo
And the corn is full grown

-1999

War and Peace

Tuesday September 11, 2001

Listen to the wind blow
Through the locust tree
Through the Russian olive leaves
Listen to the wind
Move through the piñons
And juniper
Listen as their branches sway
Into the wind's rhythm
Listen to them sigh
Listen

I hear it
Through the bedroom window
It is a gentle wind that blows
A wind allowing wind chimes
A gentle song
A quiet song
Oh   we can mourn
With gentle music
With sighs from the life
That grows around us in the ground
It all sings to what I feel
Inside me
A mourning   moving like a river
Through me   around me   as me
You feel it too

Over the cities and countrysides
Too many of us own stories to tell
And we will listen
We must listen
This is a touchstone of our history
How could evil be so evil
How can goodness   be so good
Every night follows day into night into day
And it is our time to cry
This is our time to cry

Wendy Wolff Blumberg

Aftermath

It is hard work
To not feel afraid
To have a knot hard as limestone
Push against the sanctuary walls
Of your being
Invading the sacred space
Inside you
It is hard work
To not allow it in

I will caress this fear
Sroke it as I do
The silk of Shiva's long white fur
My hand on the curve of her back
Or the soft place under her chin

Perhaps for awhile
The fear will be a part of me
Perhaps I will wear it
Like a shawl
Let it hang on the back
Of a rocking chair
To pick up or put down
As the weather changes
As the world changes
As I myself
Change

Fear
I will make it soft
Like cat fur
Soft as a shawl from Oxacca
Feel it from outside myself
And save the sacred space
Inside me
For the One
Who resides there

-September 13, 2001

Black and White

Please don't draw away your hand . . . yet.
Give me awhile longer.
Tho it could be a year or more into eternity.
Maybe not.
Keep reaching with your fingers to touch mine.
I won't give up and leave it all to you.
I promise.
So please don't draw away your hand . . . yet.

                                        -circa 1960s

Waukegan, Etc.

We wait.
Reading about Tampa and Cincinnati,
We sigh
And wordlessly wonder if the days
Stay hot
And the nights too, when will the trouble
Come here?

Very quietly
And sheltered by the soft, silent snows,
They planned.
Like generals with their strategy, they
Were thorough
And every man was given his own job
To do.

And now
That summer's heat bears down again upon
The ghetto,
They wait. With helmets and bayonets ready, they study
Mob psychology.
Winter's moments blotted up by a strengthened sun
Are lost.

Gone too
Is opportunity for words that let men know
Each other.
To penetrate hearts turned cold is warming work on
Winter days.
But they chose the other way and now, as it nears ninety
We wait too.

-1967

An Overview of the New Administration

Who will give warning this time
Is there anyone who will take the hot coals
Into his hands and throw them into the winds
And let the hot ashes fall onto the ground

There isn't any corn to feed the children now
Only stubble of stalks and hard dry skeletons of silk
If you put your ear to the ground
You will hear the far off rumble of voices
Once there was a time we could hear the corn grow
Now it is the rumble of voices that gathers the harvest
Now the rumble of discontent grows into black clouds
That pour the hailstones into our outstretched hands
That melt into nothing

There is no one to give warning
No one to listen
The rumble we hear from the earth
Has grown into a roar and spreads like lava
Over the ground
And soon the ashes from Watts and Chicago and Harlem
The hunger of children and the tears of Vietnam
Are swept away
And all that is left is the wound into which
We all will bleed

-1968

Wendy Wolff Blumberg

Riot

We'll weep, Black Sister, we'll weep together
For her whose home is dust.
Charcoaled ashes from riot weather,
A bitter wind of mistrust.
Hatred lies smoldering, pungent, and deep,
Shifting like sand.
Will she have a memory to keep
In this abounding land?
Must we, like Antigone, daughter of despair,
Live without sweet reconciliation
And beyond deeds of repair?
They've forgotten, those men of the law's creation,
Whom the law should heed.
They're not for you, Sister, so we must weep.

-1968

Hill 875

Who lies so still
Beneath a shroud
Of canvas

Black or white
Rich or poor
Man or boy

What does it
Matter now

Far away
On a hill

With
Ghosts of
Tree remains

On earth
Too parched
To bleed

You lie

I put
Three words
Beneath a
Picture
Of you

They read

Why Why Why

-1969

Wendy Wolff Blumberg

The March
On the Road to Weston

Weston is just a corn field
We don't know what we expected
To find here
But it's the Illinois prairie
Nothing more
Oh yes
A few small houses all in a row
And we wonder out loud
How the housewives survive
The winter here
So far from Chicago
Do they mourn the corn fields
And wish that giant of atomic power
Called a reactor
Had never come to change
The Midwest landscape
From the frames of their kitchen
Windows

In the land of Lincoln
They do nothing
To honor him whose ghost
Roams a wooden house
On a street paved with red brick
In Springfield
They vote No
And No

And No again
And won't make laws in 1967
For black people
To live where they want to live
Even in Weston

Now
One cold Saturday in February
A black man and I march side by side
On the road to Weston
And he tells me as he looks around
At the frozen Illinois prairie
They can keep their old corn field
It's too far from 45th Street
And I wouldn't want to live here
Anyway

-1969

Wendy Wolff Blumberg

Massive Nuclear Myocardial Infarction

When it's ninety in LA
But only seventy-five at the beach
Everyone is on the strand
With their beer and wine
After work
Watching the sun go down
South of Point Dume
Leaving the dust hued
Like Turner paints the Thames
It means walking the hill
To get to the beach
While a Brandenburg Concerto
Follows the trail of a missile
Going astray

Then
Sitting on a concrete bench
Near iceplant and sand
I watch the joggers sweat
In the Santa Ana
And the sun going down
Behind the water

Am I the only one afraid
No one
Listens

Even the surfers
Turn their backs

Peel off their wetsuits
In the parking lot
Tie their boards to the tops
Of their cars
Toss words in the air
Beer cans in the trash
And drive
Away

-1981

Wendy Wolff Blumberg

Desert Storm

This is our desert . . . here
The desert I know
The desert of early June
Driving from San Clemente
To Santa Fe
Through the Mojave
With its clumps of life
Green against dry gray dirt
And now and then an ocotillo
Its red flowers scattered
Like bows on a Christmas tree
On the ones that are in bloom
This late in spring

Across the Colorado River
The desert changes
It belongs to Arizona now
And the saguaro
The first ones are sentries
Forerunners
For their colonies that populate the hills
Leading to Wickenburg
And the mountains beyond it
That pull the road up five-thousand feet
Into Flagstaff

They are the survivors of this desert's night
The saguaro

Alive with their arms outstretched
To the sky
Or parallel to the ground
Blessing the earth
This pink and mauve and lavender earth
This fragile gift
This desert

Promise it
No tanks
No war
No oil wells

Here

-1990

South Central L. A.

Child
When sounds of gunfire and sirens
Fill the night air
That becomes your breath
Where do your dreams
Take you?

-1992

During the Riots
(Koreatown)

She rubs the side of her hand
Against her eyes
To stop the tears
From rolling down her cheeks

I don't understand
I don't understand

She says the words over and over
And it is as tho she asks a question
For which the reporter
Holding a microphone to her face
Has no answer
On the floor all around her
Lies broken glass
That reflects the camera lights
Like crystal
When she takes a few careful steps
Glass crunches under her feet
It makes a sound like footsteps
On frozen snow

-1993

Wendy Wolff Blumberg

CNN World Report

There they stand
Bunched together
The way little kids will
When they're excited
In the middle of what
Was once a street
Where shell fire and shrapnel
Make geometic chunks
Out of the pavement now
And the apartment buildings
Behind them
Into relics
Like ones I remember
From allied bombs
In a part of Florence
Near the Ponte Vecchio
Summer of 1951
But here they are
Being interviewed
Children of Sarajevo
Just children being children
In front of a camera
Even when childhood
Is broken
And cannot mend

The calm voice of an interpreter
Rolls on
Above their high pitched
Clamor

They talk   gesture   poke each other
All at the same time
Reminding me
Of a flock of noisy birds
In a tree
Until one bird voice
Clear
Like the song of a blackbird
Rises over the others
Quiets them   silences them
As the camera picks out
A face
Whose eyes look back
Into the camera's lens
While the interpreter turns Slavic
Into English
And I hear words
From this child of Sarajevo
Form a question
No one in the world
Will answer

We don't hate anyone
She says
So why can't they stop
This stupid war

Months pass
I think of them often
I bless them
And I wonder
Are they alive

-1994

Healing

Child
Put down the gun
Put it down
Hand it over to those
Who will take it apart
Bit by bit   piece by piece
Until there is a pile
Of scraps
Good for nothing at all
Except a furnace
Where metal is thrown
Into white fire
To turn itself into liquid
And then is poured
Into molds
That form nuts and bolts
Of every size
When it cools
Or nails
Large enough to build a house
Or a chain
For a playground swing

Child
If you listen carefully
You will hear the angels
Applaud your act   bless your life
You will hear the angels

Calling to your homeboys
Your homegirls
To the whole world
    Children of the Loving God
    Put down your guns
    Put them down
So put down the gun
Child
Put it down
Now

                              -1995

Wendy Wolff Blumberg

August Night

We listen to him talk
As the sun drops behind the Jemez
Setting them on fire
Their rims outlined against flames
Of coral and gold
Then blue that deepens
Shade by shade
Into cobalt near to black

A kitten plays on the ground
Around our feet
Sweet yellow corn and sunflowers grow
Along an old wood fence
Where we stand watching
While lights from Los Alamos
Across the Rio Grande
And above us the stars
Become visible one by one
Until the sky
And the hills under the mountaintops
Are filled with specks of light

His voice is pitched low
We strain to hear every word
As tho to miss even one
Would be to lose a moment
With him
The summer night

Is filled with laughter
From the party in the house
Behind us
And the far off bark
Of a dog

    Do you see those lights
    Over there

He raises his hand towards Los Alamos

    I spent fourteen years
    There
    I didn't know what they were doing
    Didn't know
    Everything I learned
    I learned from experience
    Not from books
    I learned from the earth
    And from my people
    And I know
    War destroys
    And is cruel
    The Indian people
    Worship Earth
    And I say to you
    Young people
    You must learn to do
    The same
    History repeats
    I ask you why
    The people of the earth

Wendy Wolff Blumberg

Cannot get along
Peace must come
To Earth

Twenty years go by
He is gone for half of them
The stars and Los Alamos
Remain in their places
Corn and sunflowers still grow
From the earth of northern New Mexico
And in the world
History repeats
As war destroys
And is cruel

-Written during NATO bombing Yugoslovia
and ethnic cleansing in Kosovo, April 1999,
from an experience of the 1970s

Last Page
October 20, 2001

Like tall sailing ships
Clouds move slowly from the west
Gray billows
Reaching far up into the sky
Over Santa Fe
Before their rain begins
A robin finds the birdbath
Sits in the water
As a king would on his throne
Then splashes himself with his wings
Hops to a branch of the piñon tree
Shakes off his bath
Flies away

These are the things
That clothe my life
Moments that pass quickly
Seen with my eyes   heard with my ears
Felt in my heart
My life is filled with people I love
People I don't know
Animals I love
Animals I don't know
I feel connected to it all
And so   I write a poem